iRish BLESSiNGS

Designed by Tony and Penny Mills

irish
BLESSINGS

This edition published and distributed by Tara, 1999

Tara is an imprint of Parragon

Parragon
Queen Street House
4 Queen Street
Bath BA1 1HE

Produced by Magpie Books, an imprint of
Robinson Publishing Ltd, London

ISBN 1 90287 901 5

A copy of the British Library Cataloguing-in-Publication Data is available
from the British Library

Printed in China

ACKNOWLEDGEMENTS

Pictures on pp 5, 25, and 42 are by courtesy of Mr Paul O'Hanlan and
those on pp 9, 15, 19, 27, 28, 32, 33, 34, 37, 39, 45 and 47 have been
very kindly supplied by Celia Haddon.
We have been unable to trace the owners of certain copyrights and beg
forgiveness of anyone whose rights have been overlooked.

CONTENTS

INTRODUCTION

Ireland is famously a land of saints. It was, of course, St Patrick who brought Christianity to Ireland, and in its train there followed a common learning and culture that bound together its people. Religion and a belief in a good and gracious God have provided a refuge and a consolation to the Irish in times of trouble, and an awareness of God's providence in times of good fortune.

However, the natural good spirits of the Irish have provided a good leavening of humour and jollity to most occasions, and this selection of sayings reflects not only the deeper and more serious side of Irish life but also the wit and repartée that are never long absent from any social gathering.

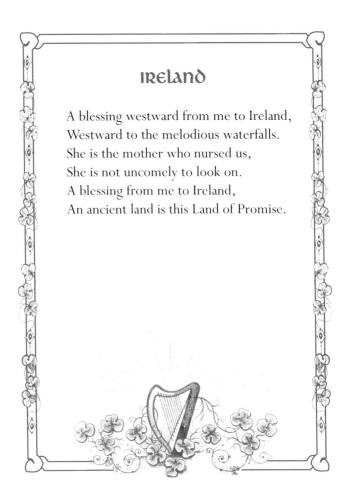

IReLAND

A blessing westward from me to Ireland,
Westward to the melodious waterfalls.
She is the mother who nursed us,
She is not uncomely to look on.
A blessing from me to Ireland,
An ancient land is this Land of Promise.

Yet, oh! if spirits can e'er leave the
   appointed place of rest,
Once more I will revisit thee, dear Isle that
   I love best,
O'er thy green vales will hover slow,
And many a parting blessing will bestow.

May the air bless you, and water and the
wind, the sea, and all the hours of the sun
and moon.

J.M. SYNGE
Deirdre of the Sorrows

Wherever you go and whatever you do,
May the luck of the Irish
be there with you.

longevity

May I see you grey
and combing your
grandchildren's hair.

May God grant you many years to live,
For sure he must be knowing,
The earth has angels all too few,
And heaven is overflowing.

May you live long,
Die happy,
And rate a mansion in heaven.

Long life to you, a wet mouth,
and death in
Ireland.

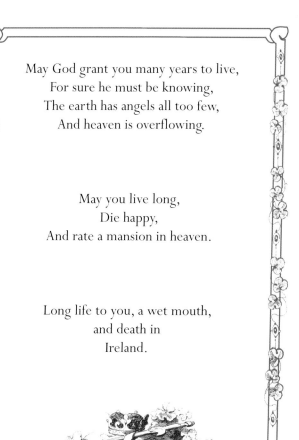

May you live as long as you want,
And never want as long as you live.

May you live to be a hundred years,
With one extra year to repent!

May the Good Lord take a liking to you,
but not too soon!

May you die in bed at ninety-five years,
Shot by a jealous wife!

happiness

May your troubles be less
And your blessings be more.
And nothing but happiness
Come through your door.

May every gentle wind that blows
Send happiness to you.

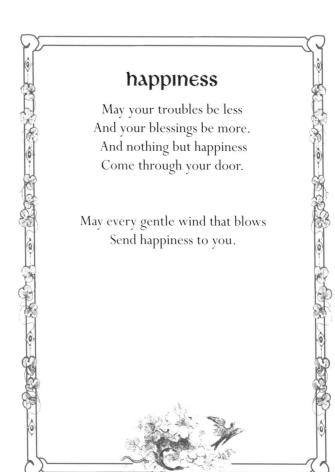

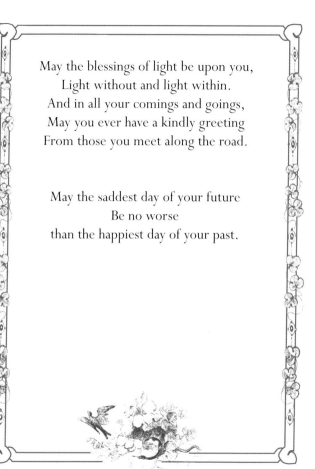

May the blessings of light be upon you,
Light without and light within.
And in all your comings and goings,
May you ever have a kindly greeting
From those you meet along the road.

May the saddest day of your future
Be no worse
than the happiest day of your past.

peace

I wish the citizens of Heaven in this house,
And vessels of peace to be given to them.

Deep peace of the running wave to you,
Deep peace of the flowing air to you,
Deep peace of the quiet earth to you,
Deep peace of the shining stars to you,
Deep peace of the Son of Peace to you.

good fortune

I wish you a small cabin,
but not too small.

May the most you wish for
Be the least you get.

Good health, good luck, and happiness,
For today and every day.

May your pockets be heavy
and your heart be light.
May good luck pursue you
each morning and night.

May the face of every good news,
And the back of every bad news,
Be toward us.

May you live all the days of your life.

JONATHAN SWIFT

May you taste the sweetest pleasures that
fortune has bestowed.

GETTING UP

At the break of the day the cockerel calls
    'Get up! Get up! and leave thy bed,
    If you the way of God would tread
There is much to be done ere evening falls'.

For the blessing of God on them does alight
Who follow his course, both by day and
    by night.

Through all the day watch over me,
  Lord God, who reignest high,
You know how little I am worth;
  Without Thee I am nought.

Be Thou with me through the night,
And bring me at last to Thy great light.

GOING OUT

God the Father be with you,
　　When you go out today;
Jesus, Son of Holy Mary,
　　Watch you on your way;
O Holy Spirit, Comforter,
　　Bring you safe home at close of day.

God of the Winds! O hear my pray'r,
    Safe passage now bestow!
Soft, o'er the slumbering deep, may fair
    And prosperous breezes flow!
O'er the rough rock and swelling wave,
    Do thou our progress guide,
Do thou from angry ocean save,
    And o'er its rage preside.

at work

May there always be work
for your hands to do,
May your purse always hold
a coin or two.
May the sun always shine warm
on your windowpane,
May a rainbow be certain
to follow each rain.
May the hand of a friend
always be near you,
And may God fill your heart
with gladness to cheer you.

May the saints be surprised
at your success.

The blessings of God be on your farm,
  On your pigs and on your cow;
And may St Michael guard from harm
  Your crops, your fields and grain
  in store.
And dear St Bridget, give peace and calm
  To all who work this land of thine.

May you have:
No frost on your spuds,
No worms on your cabbage,
May your goat give plenty of milk.
And if you inherit a donkey,
May she be in foal.

May the luck of the Irish
Lead to happiest heights,
And the highway you travel
Be lined with green lights.

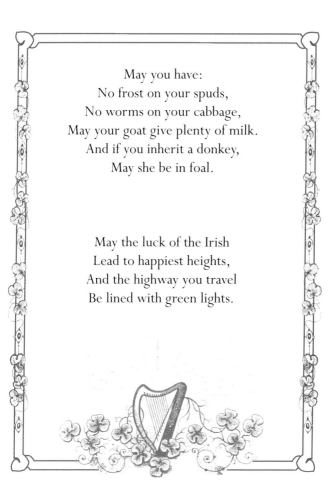

grace at meals

O God, who took five loaves and two
fishes,
And with them fed five thousand,
Who has given us the food on this table
To savour and enjoy,
Give your blessing to all gathered here,
And guide us in all we do and say.

Every time we sit and eat,
Let us give thanks to God above
For our bread and for our meat.

It is God who loads our table,
Whom we praise, whom we adore.

GOING TO BED

May God bless you, my child,
May he watch over you and protect you
This night and every night to come.
May rich blessings accompany you,
Friends ever go with you,
Troubles avoid you.
Whether rich or poor, wherever you fare,
May happiness surround you, now and
    ever more.

comfort & friendship

May you have:
A world of wishes at your command,
God and his angels close at hand,
Friends and family their love impart,
And Irish blessings in your heart!

May your neighbours respect you,
Trouble neglect you,
The angels protect you,
And heaven accept you.

May you have food and raiment,
A soft pillow for your head,
May you be forty years in heaven,
Before the devil knows you're dead.

May you have warm words
on a cold evening,
A full moon on a dark night,
And the road downhill
all the way to your door.

Blessings on the man
who invented poteen.

May the roof above us never fall in,
And may the friends gathered below it
never fall out.

May those who love us, love us.
And those that don't love us,
May God turn their hearts.
And if He doesn't turn their hearts,
May he turn their ankles,
So we'll know them by their limping.

May your right hand always
Be stretched out in friendship,
And never in want.

May the Lord make a bed
in Glory for you.

wedding blessings

May your mornings bring joy,
And your evenings bring peace.
May your troubles grow few,
As your blessings increase.

May your hands
be forever clasped in friendship,
And your hearts
joined forever in love.

May there be a generation of children
On the children of
your children.

May joy and peace surround you,
Contentment latch your door,
And happiness be with you now
And bless you evermore.

May you get all your wishes but one,
So you always have something
to strive for!

May God be with you and bless you.
May you see your children's children.
May you be poor in misfortune,
rich in blessings.
May you know nothing but happiness
From this day forward.

Health and long life to you.
Land without rent to you.
A child every year to you.
And if you can't go to heaven,
May you at least die in Ireland.

christmas

May peace and plenty be the first
To lift the latch on your door,
And happiness be guided to your home
By the candle of Christmas.

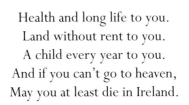

49

A Few Irish Curses

May you leave without returning.

May the cat eat you, and may the cat be
eaten by the devil.

Six eggs to you,
And half a dozen of them rotten.

The devil go with you and sixpence,
And then you will want neither money
nor company.

You'll sup sorrow for this.

May you melt off the earth,
Like snow off the ditch.

May you melt like butter before
a summer sun.

May the devil make a ladder of
your backbone,
While he is picking apples in
the garden of Hell.

May you rot on the hills,
That the crows may feed
upon your carcass!

Die! an' give the crow a puddin'.

The devil's luck to you.

BLessings from
saint patrick

May St Patrick guard you wherever
you go and guide you in
whatever you do – and may his loving
protection be a blessing to you always.

May the road rise to meet you,
May the wind be always at your back,
May the sun shine warm upon your face,
The rains fall soft upon your fields,
And until we meet again,
May God hold you
in the palm of His hand.

May the leprechauns be near you
To spread luck along your way.
And may all the Irish angels,
Smile upon you
on St Patrick's Day.

"And its O, the green Shamrock"

God watch over you, on you way;
And bring you safely to the end of the day.